VOLCANOES

Nature's Incredible Fireworks

by David L. Harrison

Illustrated by Cheryl Nathan

Boyds Mills Press

The author wishes to thank Erwin J. Mantei, Ph.D., Professor of Geology,
Southwest Missouri State University, for his review of the original manuscript.

Published by Boyds Mills Press, Inc.
A Highlights Company
815 Church Street
Honesdale, Pennsylvania 18431
Printed in China
Visit our Web site at www.boydsmillspress.com

Publisher Cataloging-in-Publication Data (U.S.)

Harrison, David L.
Volcanoes: nature's incredible fireworks / by David L. Harrison;
illustrated by Cheryl Nathan.—1st ed.
[32] p. : col. ill. ; cm.
Summary: A basic examination of how volcanoes are formed.
ISBN 1-56397-996-9
1. Volcanoes—Juvenile literature. (1. Volcanoes.) I. Nathan, Cheryl. II. Title.
551.21 21 2002 CIP QE522.P75
2001094536

First edition, 2002
The text of this book is set in 18-point Optima.

10 9 8 7 6 5 4 3 2 1

In memory of two special teachers,
Laura Bond and Clark Graham,
for a gift I can never repay.

— D. L. H.

For my brother, Donald Nathan.

— C. N.

Earth is never still.
Every day somewhere
it trembles and quivers.
Every day somewhere
volcanoes erupt.
From far off
they look like
beautiful fireworks.

But up close,
a volcano is no fun.
What looks like sparks
are fiery blobs
of melted rock
called lava.

Gases and geysers
of scalding hot steam,
ground-up rocks,
and gritty ashes
blast into the air
and turn the sky dark.

If too much gas
is trapped inside,
part of the mountain
may blow off,
hurling rocks
heavier than elephants
for miles.
Some explosions
cause floods,
mud slides,
and avalanches
that roar downhill,
destroying everything
in their path.

But not all volcanoes explode.
If enough gas escapes first,
red rivers of lava flow out
through the cracks and crevices.

Some kinds of lava
ooze and slide slowly.
Others stream down the mountain
as quickly as cars in city traffic.

Outer core

Inner core

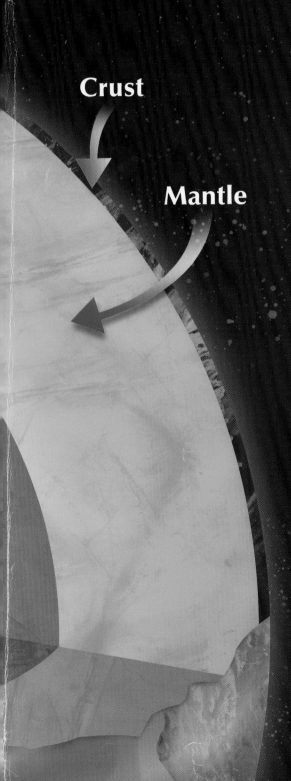

Crust

Mantle

How do rocks
get so hot they melt?
What causes volcanoes?
The answers lie deep
beneath our feet
in the four parts
of the earth —
the crust,
the mantle,
the outer core,
and the inner core.

The crust, where we live,
is covered by land and oceans.
In places under the seas
the crust is only
three miles deep.
It may be forty-three miles thick
beneath the mountains.

Below the crust,
the mantle stretches down
1800 miles.
Rocks there melt
to a gooey paste or tar
called magma.

The core is a huge ball
more than 2100 miles
to its center.
It is mostly iron so hot that
the outer core is liquid.
But the inner core is solid.
Pressure there is so great
it keeps the iron from melting.

Crust

Mantle

Outer core

Inner core

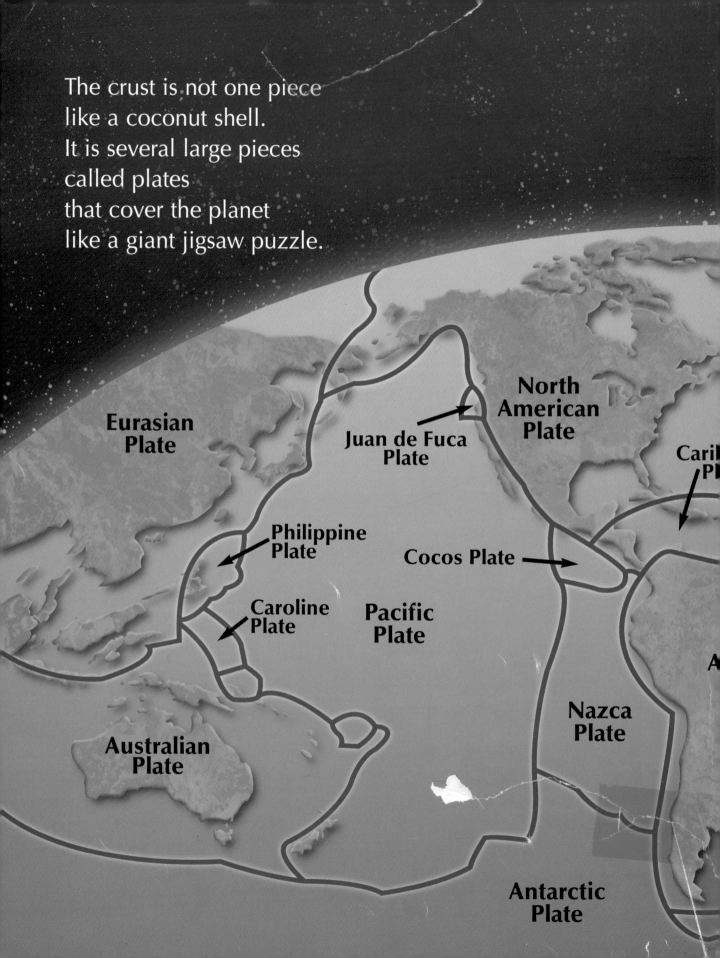

The crust is not one piece
like a coconut shell.
It is several large pieces
called plates
that cover the planet
like a giant jigsaw puzzle.

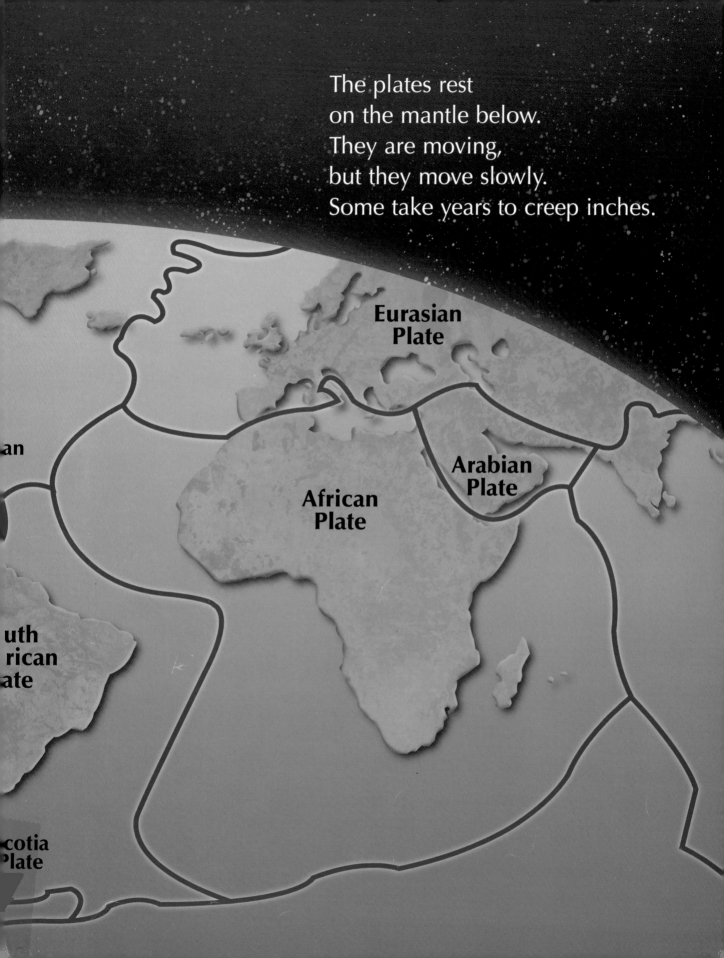

The plates rest
on the mantle below.
They are moving,
but they move slowly.
Some take years to creep inches.

Eurasian
Plate

Arabian
Plate

African
Plate

an

uth
rican
ate

cotia
Plate

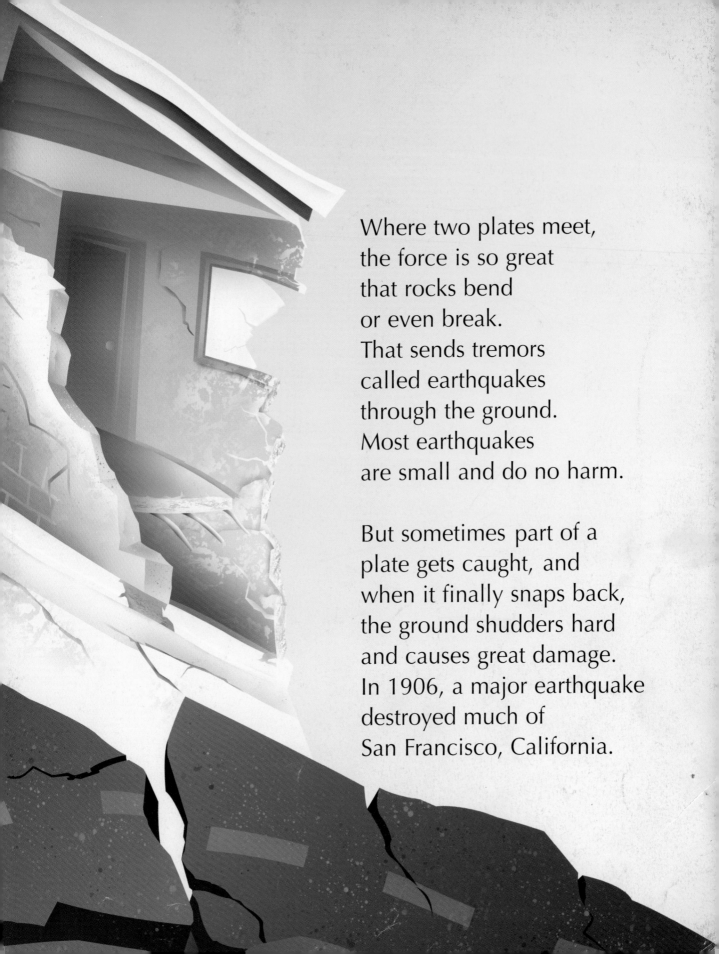

Where two plates meet,
the force is so great
that rocks bend
or even break.
That sends tremors
called earthquakes
through the ground.
Most earthquakes
are small and do no harm.

But sometimes part of a
plate gets caught, and
when it finally snaps back,
the ground shudders hard
and causes great damage.
In 1906, a major earthquake
destroyed much of
San Francisco, California.

Most magma moves
toward the crust
where it cools
and sinks again.
But some magma
breaks through weak spots
by rising through cracks
like chimney flues
until at last it bubbles
or blasts free
onto the surface.

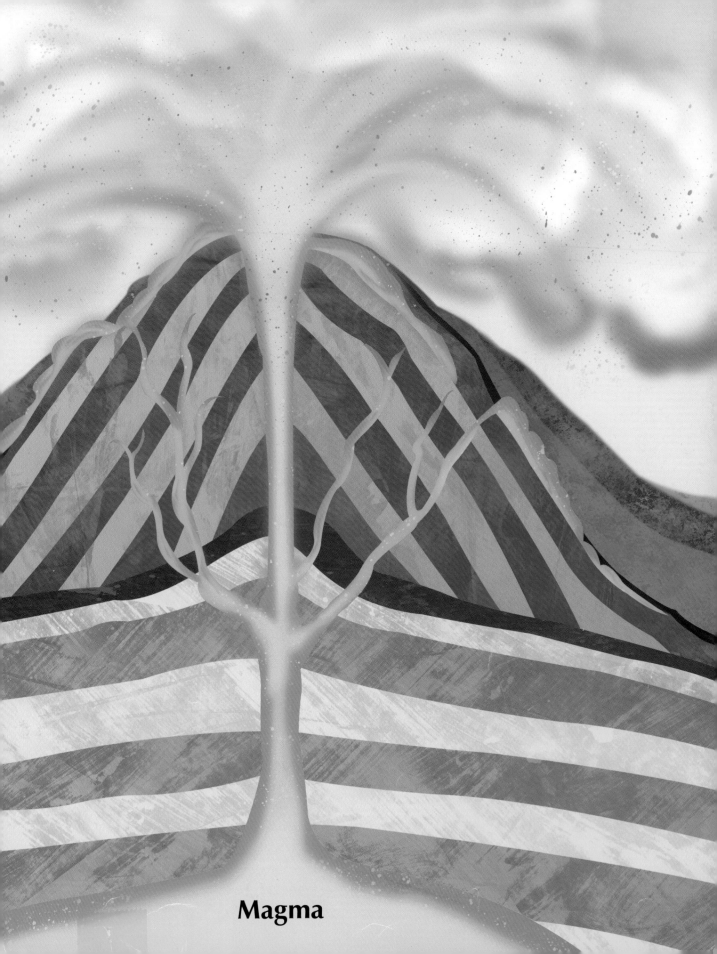

Magma

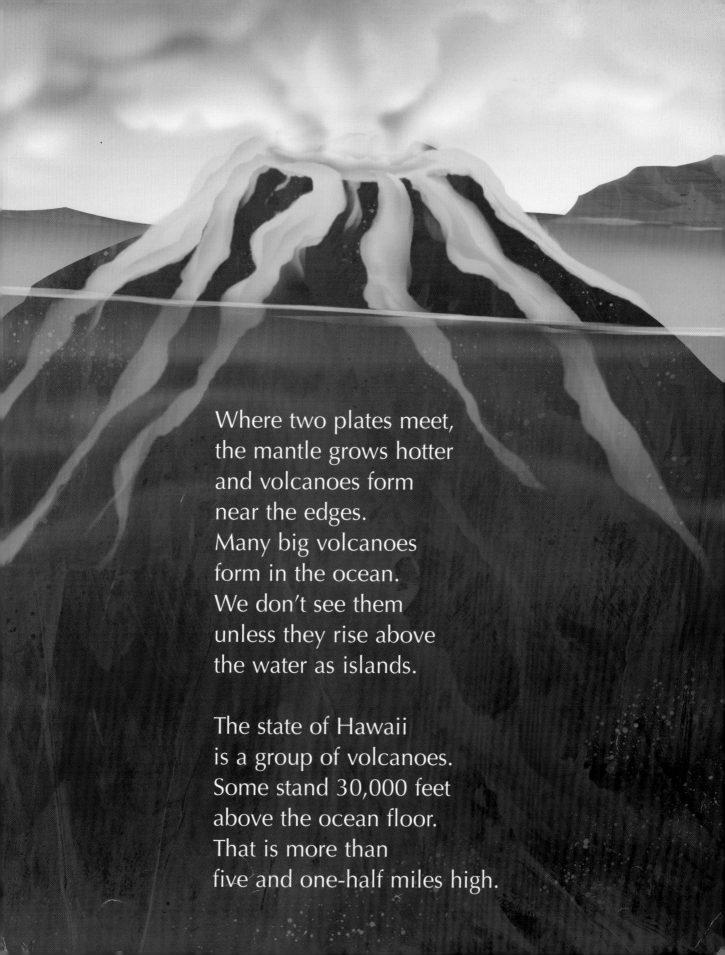

Where two plates meet,
the mantle grows hotter
and volcanoes form
near the edges.
Many big volcanoes
form in the ocean.
We don't see them
unless they rise above
the water as islands.

The state of Hawaii
is a group of volcanoes.
Some stand 30,000 feet
above the ocean floor.
That is more than
five and one-half miles high.

Around the Pacific Ocean,
so many plates collide
with one another that
many of the world's
greatest eruptions
have happened there.
We call it the Ring of Fire.

In the United States,
Mount St. Helens
erupted in 1980
with such force that part
of the mountain expoded.

One of the most famous
volcanoes in history
is Mount Vesuvius in Italy.
When it erupted in AD 79,
it buried the cities of
Pompeii and Herculaneum
under ash, mud, and lava.

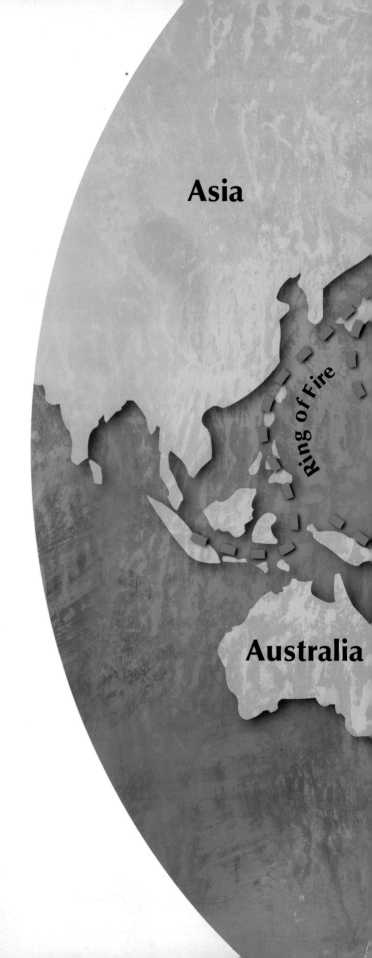

Asia

Ring of Fire

Australia

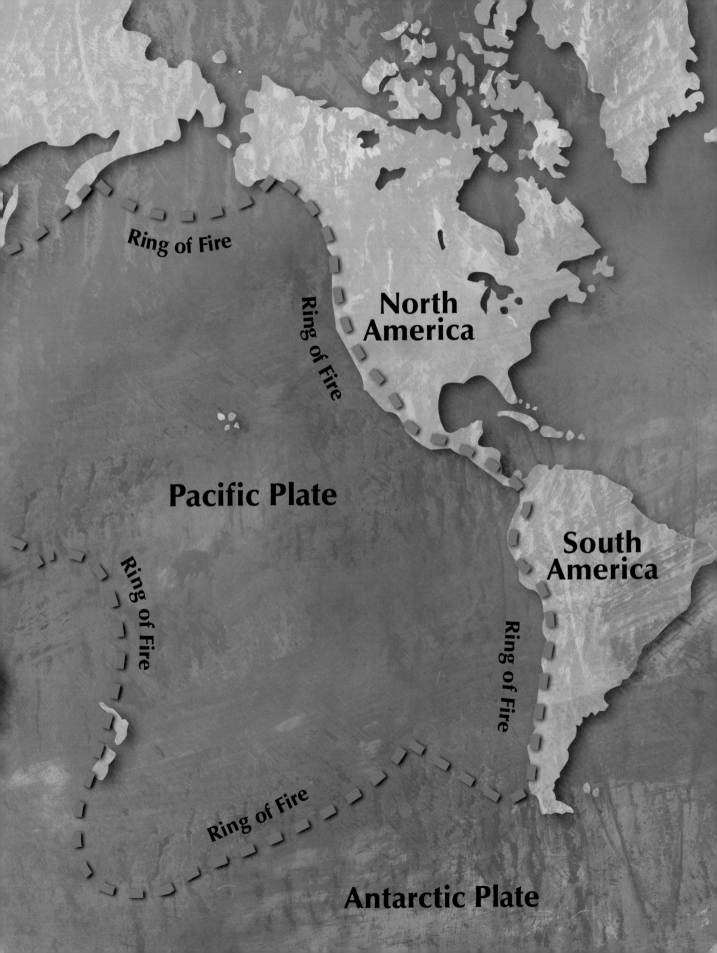

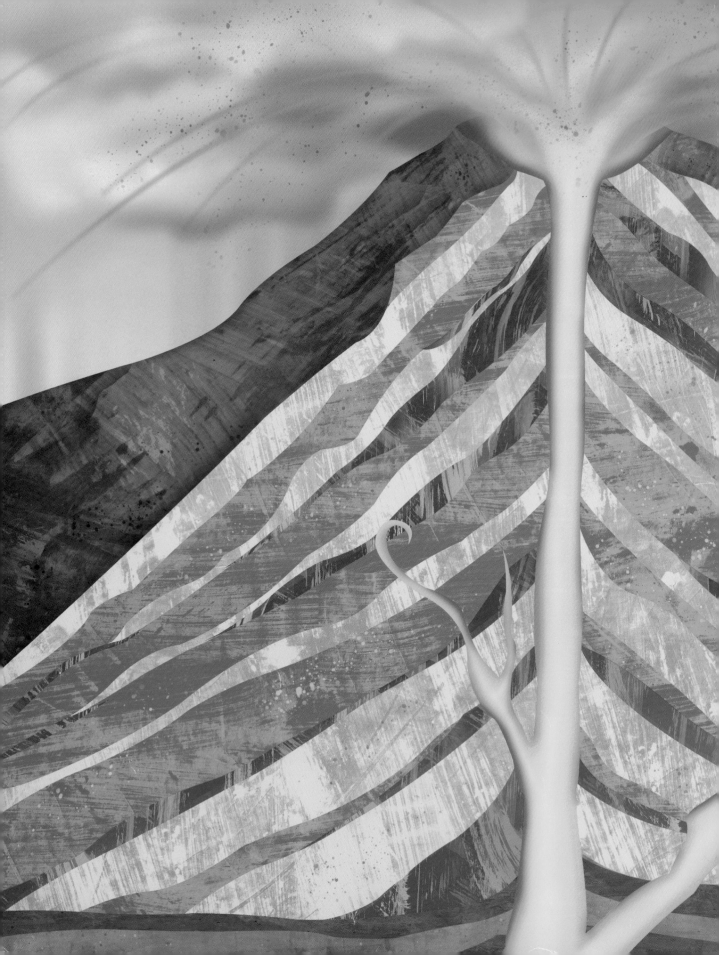

Over thousands of years,
a volcano may erupt
again and again.
Between eruptions,
it may sleep in silence
for long periods.

After each eruption,
lava cools into rock,
and ash settles to the ground.
Layers of lava and ash
slowly build the volcano
until it becomes a tall mountain.

As new magma pushes
against the surface,
rocks move and the
ground shakes.
These earthquakes
help us know
the volcano may be
getting ready to erupt.

We study volcanoes to learn
when a sleeping giant
may suddenly awaken
to belch hot gasses
and spit out fiery lava.

Scientists are learning
what causes volcanoes
and how they erupt.

We still can't predict
when the next volcano
will blow its top
or split its sides.

But three things
we know for sure.
Volcanoes are beautiful.
They are dangerous.
And they are nature's
incredible fireworks.

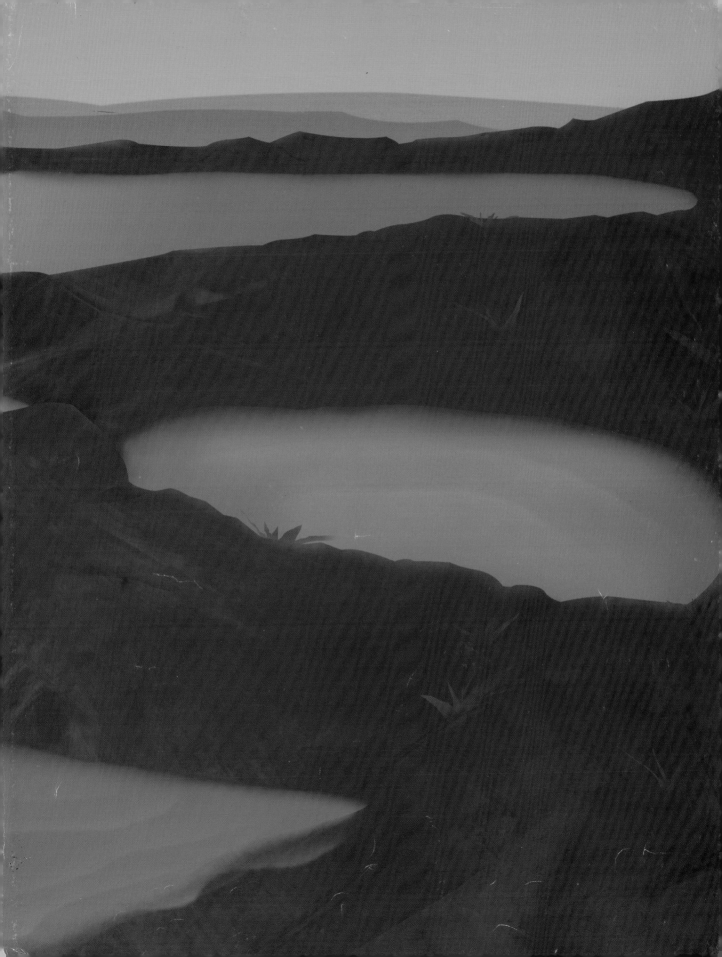

AUTHOR'S NOTE

There is much we don't yet understand about volcanoes and earthquakes. They both result from natural forces at and below the earth's surface, and we cannot go inside our planet to look for ourselves. No drill we can make would survive the heat even a few miles down. So what we know and think we know depends on what we can see, measure, and analyze on the surface. Knowledge begins with questions.

How can solid rock bend and fold or snap in two? What force is so powerful it makes the ground shudder and quake? The answer is that our planet is covered with enormous plates of rock moving against, over, and under one another, and their slow-motion crashes and fender benders can shake the ground for hundreds of miles.

How can there be a line of volcanoes miles apart with only one—the newest—still active? The answer might be that far beneath the surface lies a vast supply of molten rock. Sometimes, after long periods of boiling and churning, the molten rock moves upward until it explodes through the crust in a fiery geyser of ash and lava. But what if the plate above this "hot spot" has moved on since the last eruption? The old cone now sits miles away like a burned-out Fourth of July fountain, so the new eruption breaks through the surface to form a new volcano.

Volcanic eruptions and earthquakes do not always develop in the same place or at the same time. Yet it is hard to talk about one without the other. That is why this book includes both subjects. I hope this introduction to the mysteries and the amazing power of volcanoes and earthquakes whets your appetite to learn more about them. Here is a list of good books you can read.

—**David L. Harrison**

FURTHER READING

Berger, Melvin, et al. *Why Do Volcanoes Blow Their Tops?: Questions and Answers About Volcanoes & Earthquakes*. New York: Scholastic, 1999.

Drohan, Michael. *Volcanoes*. New York: Powerkids Press, 1999.

Dudman, John. *Volcano*. New York: Thomson Learning, 1993.

Furgang, Kathy. *Mount Vesuvius: Europe's Mighty Volcano of Smoke and Ash*. New York: Powerkids Press, 2000.

Ganeri, Anita. *Volcanoes*. London: Dorling Kindersley, 2001.

Halley, Ned. *Disasters*. New York: Kingfisher Publications, 1999.

Nirgiotis, Nicholas. *Volcanoes: Mountains that Blow Their Tops*. New York: Grosset & Dunlap, 1996.

Walker, Sally. *Volcanoes: Earth's Inner Fire*. Minneapolis, Minnesota: Carolrhoda Books, 1994.